Q Goes to Curly Land

Valerie Jerome

Illustrated by: Jessica Stevenson

Copyright © 2019 Valerie Jerome
Illustrated by Jessica Stevenson
All rights reserved.

No part of this book may be reproduced in any manner without the written consent of the publisher except for brief excerpts in critical reviews or articles.

ISBN: 978-1-61244-762-9
Library of Congress Control Number: 2019909731

Printed in the United States of America

Halo Publishing International
1100 NW Loop 410
Suite 700 - 176
San Antonio, Texas 78213
www.halopublishing.com
contact@halopublishing.com

For my daughters, Tavia and Amara.

Born with coily brown curls,
Q makes other heads whirl.

Twisted, braided, or down, they bounce;
Q mostly loves each ounce.

With a mind of their own,
they sometimes make Q groan.

So she puts them up high
and then lets out a deep sigh.

Her sister says, "Let them loose!" and so the girls make a truce.

They imagine a place where curls have their own space.

They name this new world Curly Land.
It is wild, bright, and grand.

Here, they care for their curls.

Feeling happy, the girls twirl.

While looking around,
they find a curl power potion
that coats their locks with lotion.

A wacky roller comb stands at the ready in a dome.

It unties pesky knots, gliding from spot to spot.

There are no more tangles.
The sisters stand strong and able.

Q knows that her curls are truly great.
She does not want them straight.

With styles from which to choose,
Q knows she cannot lose.

Wavy, kinky, or curly,
curly-haired girls are worthy.

On this hair journey,
the girls are living, loving, learning.

Mom calls from down the street.
It is time to go eat!

23

Their daydream has ended, but the trip was splendid.

She is one-of-a-kind
with her curls and her sharp mind.

www.ingramcontent.com/pod-product-compliance
Lightning Source LLC
Chambersburg PA
CBHW041439040426
42453CB00021B/2461